Your Legacy of Love: 101 Ways to Leave a Lasting Legacy

Practical Steps to Ensure Your Family's Future and Preserve Your Values

Lisa Drew Ed.D

Copyright © 2024 by Lisa Drew

All rights reserved. No part of this book may be reproduced, distributed, or transmitted in any form or by any means, including photocopying, recording, or other electronic or mechanical methods, without the prior written permission of the publisher, except in the case of brief quotations embodied in critical reviews and certain other noncommercial uses permitted by copyright law.

Disclaimer

This book is intended for **entertainment and educational purposes only**. This book is designed to provide general information on the topics of emotional and financial legacy planning. The content is intended for educational and informational purposes only and should not be considered as financial, legal, or professional advice. Readers are encouraged to consult with qualified professionals, such as financial advisors, estate planners, or attorneys, to address their specific circumstances and create customized plans that align with their goals and needs.

The suggestions and examples provided herein are illustrative and may not be applicable to all situations. Decisions regarding life insurance, estate planning, or financial investments should be made with careful consideration of individual needs, financial conditions, and the guidance of licensed professionals.

The authors and publishers disclaim any liability for actions taken based on the information presented in this book. Laws and regulations related to financial and estate planning may vary by jurisdiction and are subject to change. Readers are encouraged to seek up-to-date advice to ensure compliance with relevant laws and policies.

By using this book, readers acknowledge that the responsibility for making informed decisions rests solely with them and that this book is not a substitute for professional advice.

Permissions Requests
Requests to the publisher for permissions should be addressed to:
2227 Old Bridge Rd Woodbridge, VA. 22192 info@redcarpetbusinessexpo.com

Published by Lisa Drew 2227 Old Bridge Rd Woodbridge, VA. 22192
Printed in the U.S.

Table Of Contents

Introduction	8
Chapter 1: Emotional Gifts for Your Family	12
1. Write a Legacy Letter: Share Your Values, Dreams, and Wisdom	18
2. Record Personal Video Messages: Leave Heartfelt Words for Special Occasions	19
3. Create a Family Photo Book: Highlight Cherished Memories and Milestones	20
4. Pass Down Meaningful Heirlooms: Attach Stories to Treasured Items	21
5. Share Lessons Learned from Your Life Journey: Help Guide Future Generations	22
Chapter 2: Life Insurance—Your Legacy's Cornerstone	23
6. Purchase a Life Insurance Policy: Ensure Your Loved Ones Have Financial Stability	24
7. Choose the Right Coverage Amount: Calculate Your Family's Future Needs	25
8. Understand Term vs. Whole Life Insurance: Choose What Aligns with Your Long-Term Goals	26
9. Add a Final Expense Policy: Cover Funeral Costs and Eliminate Financial Stress for Your Family	27
10. Review Your Policy Regularly: Ensure It Reflects Any Life Changes	28
Chapter 3: Planning for Final Expenses	29
11. Prepay Funeral Expenses: Lock in Costs and Ease Financial Pressure on Loved Ones	31
12. Create a Funeral Plan: Document Your Wishes for Services, Burial, or Cremation	32
13. Research Funeral Insurance: A Dedicated Policy Ensures All Final Costs Are Covered	33
14. Choose a Trusted Beneficiary: Select Someone Responsible to Manage Final Arrangements	34
15. Include Obituary Funds in Your Plan: Cover the Cost of a Meaningful Memorial Announcement	35
Chapter 4: Financial Stability for Loved Ones	36
16. Create a Financial Blueprint for Your Family: Outline Your Current and Future Assets	37
17. Use Life Insurance to Pay Off Debts: Avoid Leaving Unpaid Loans or Credit Card Balances	38
18. Set Up an Education Fund: Provide for Children or Grandchildren's College Expenses	39
19. Consider a Joint Life Insurance Policy: Cover Both You and Your Spouse Under One Plan	40
20. Ensure Coverage for Long-Term Care: Life Insurance Riders Can Help with Medical or Elder Care Costs	41
Chapter 5: Estate Planning Made Simple	42
21. Write a Comprehensive Will: Outline Your Wishes for Property and Assets	43
22. Establish a Living Trust: Protect Your Assets and Avoid Probate	44
23. Update Your Life Insurance Beneficiaries: Ensure They Reflect Your Current Relationships	45

24. Name a Power of Attorney: Choose Someone to Handle Finances if You Become Incapacitated   46
25. Document Your Digital Assets: Include Passwords and Online Account Details for Easy Access   47

Chapter 6: Protecting Your Legacy with Insurance: A Blueprint for Peace of Mind   48

26. Invest in Permanent Life Insurance: Build Cash Value While Securing Future Benefits   49
27. Consider Burial Insurance: Specifically Designed to Cover End-of-Life Expenses   50
28. Explore Accidental Death Policies: Add Extra Protection for Unforeseen Events   51
29. Add Critical Illness Riders: Ensure Coverage if You Face Serious Health Challenges   52
30. Bundle Policies for Savings: Combine Life, Health, and Burial Insurance for Better Rates   53

Chapter 7: Securing a Debt-Free Future   54

31. Use Life Insurance to Cover Mortgages: Prevent Your Family From Losing Their Home   55
32. Pay Off Car Loans With Insurance Proceeds: Remove Additional Burdens   56
33. Eliminate Lingering Medical Bills: Ensure No Debts Remain Unpaid   57
34. Provide for Final Utility and Tax Payments: Avoid Unexpected Costs for Your Heirs   58
35. Include Funds for Estate Taxes: Large Estates May Require Additional Coverage   59

Chapter 8: Supporting End-of-Life Decisions   60

36. Create an Advance Directive: Outline Your Medical Care Preferences   61
37. Discuss Your Wishes With Loved Ones: Avoid Misunderstandings During Difficult Times   62
38. Appoint a Healthcare Proxy: Select Someone You Trust to Make Medical Decisions   63
39. Include End-of-Life Care in Your Insurance Plan: Consider Policies That Cover Hospice and Palliative Care   64
40. Document Burial or Cremation Preferences: Provide Clarity and Peace of Mind   65

Chapter 9: Leveraging Life Insurance for Legacy Projects   66

41. Fund Scholarships or Education Trusts: Create Opportunities for Future Generations   67
42. Support Charitable Causes: Name a Nonprofit as a Beneficiary   68
43. Provide a Financial Cushion for Your Spouse: Ensure They Can Live Comfortably After Your Passing   69
44. Help Your Children or Grandchildren Buy Homes: Allocate Part of Your Insurance Benefits for Housing   70
45. Leave a Lasting Family Fund: Establish a Resource for Emergencies or Celebrations   71

Chapter 10: Practical Planning for Loved Ones   72

46. Leave Clear Instructions for Accessing Insurance Benefits: Help Beneficiaries File Claims Easily   73

47. Compile a "Legacy Binder": Include Policies, Accounts, and Instructions   74
48. Educate Your Family on Financial Literacy: Empower Them to Manage Your Gifts Wisely   75
49. Create an Emergency Fund Through Insurance Savings: Prepare for Unexpected Needs   76
50. Assign a Trusted Advisor: Guide Your Family Through Financial and Legal Processes   77

Chapter 11: Ensuring Financial Wellness for Generations   78
51. Establish Multi-Generational Wealth With Whole Life Insurance: Build Lasting Financial Security   79
52. Gift Annual Premiums for Policies on Your Children: Start Their Coverage Early   80
53. Ensure Retirement Funds for Your Spouse: Supplement Social Security or Pensions   81
54. Offer Down-Payment Assistance for Future Homes: Help Family Members Build Stability   82
55. Provide for Family Travel or Reunions: Ensure Bonds Remain Strong   83

Chapter 12: Reducing the Burden of Final Expenses   84
56. Specify Headstone and Burial Costs in Your Policy: Eliminate Guesswork   85
57. Cover Memorial Service Expenses: Include Venue, Catering, and Flowers   86
58. Set Aside Travel Funds for Attending Family: Make It Easier for Loved Ones to Gather   87
59. Plan for Legal Fees Associated With Settling Your Estate: Avoid Surprises   88
60. Ensure Transportation of Remains If Needed: Include Costs for Relocation   89

Chapter 13: Teaching Financial Preparedness   90
61. Teach Your Children About Life Insurance: Help Them Understand Its Value   91
62. Encourage Budgeting and Saving Early: Financial Literacy Is a Gift   92
63. Show Them How to Invest Wisely: Set the Example With Your Policies   93
64. Discuss Emergency Planning Openly: Normalize Preparation   94
65. Pass Down a Philosophy of Financial Responsibility: Lead by Example   95

Chapter 14: Preserving Your Memory   96
66. Create a Family Video Library: Share Stories, Wisdom, and Laughter   97
67. Host a Living Celebration: Share Love and Gratitude While Alive   98
68. Plant a Tree in Your Honor: A Living Symbol of Your Legacy   99
69. Write a Book or Memoir: Document Your Life Lessons   100
70. Dedicate a Family Tradition in Your Name: Keep Your Memory Alive Through Shared Experiences   101

Chapter 15: Passing on Values Alongside Wealth   102
71. Tie Insurance Benefits to Meaningful Goals: Encourage Recipients to Use Funds for Education, Homeownership, or Investments   103
72. Include a Letter of Intent With Your Insurance Policy: Explain Your Hopes for How the Money Will Be Used   104
73. Establish a Family Mission Statement: Use Your Legacy to Reflect Shared Values   105

74. Encourage Philanthropy With a Portion of the Benefits: Teach the Importance of Giving Back — 106
75. Create a Family Trust Fund With Guidelines for Use: Ensure Your Wealth Supports Future Generations Responsibly — 107

Chapter 16: Empowering Your Beneficiaries — 108

76. Prepare Your Family to Handle Life Insurance Claims: Provide Step-by-Step Instructions — 109
77. Teach Them About Tax Implications of Receiving Benefits: Help Them Plan Wisely — 110
78. Appoint a Financial Advisor to Guide Them: Ensure They Have Support for Smart Decisions — 111
79. Include Beneficiaries in Legacy Planning Discussions: Foster Transparency and Trust — 112
80. Ensure They Understand Your Life Insurance Policy Details: Avoid Confusion or Missed Opportunities — 113

Chapter 17: Long-Term Impact Through Life Insurance — 114

81. Set Up Policies for Younger Family Members: Protect Them While Building Cash Value — 115
82. Use Life Insurance as a Retirement Tool: Policies With Living Benefits Can Supplement Income — 116
83. Create a Lasting Charitable Endowment: Use Your Policy to Fund Causes You Care About — 117
84. Provide for Unexpected Expenses for Generations to Come: Build a Financial Cushion — 118
85. Turn Insurance Benefits Into Investment Opportunities: Encourage Heirs to Grow the Wealth You Leave Behind — 119

Chapter 18: The Role of Communication in Legacy Planning — 120

86. Discuss Your Plans Openly With Loved Ones: Eliminate Uncertainty and Misunderstanding — 121
87. Host a Family Legacy Meeting: Share Your Intentions and Invite Questions — 122
88. Write a "Legacy Letter" for Family Members: Personalize Your Messages to Each Recipient — 123
89. Encourage Feedback During Planning: Let Family Members Feel Involved in the Process — 124
90. Create a Digital Legacy Plan: Share Access to Important Online Accounts and Documents — 125

Chapter 19: Leaving a Lasting Emotional Impact — 126

91. Write Goodbye Letters for Significant Life Milestones: Birthdays, Weddings, or Other Key Moments — 127
92. Create a Time Capsule With Personal Mementos: Include Photos, Letters, and Cherished Items — 128
93. Start a Family Tradition in Your Honor: Let Your Memory Live On in Shared Rituals — 129
94. Record Your Voice or Create Videos: Hearing and Seeing You Will Bring Comfort to Your Loved Ones — 130

95. Celebrate Life's Milestones Together While You Can: Leave No Regrets in the Hearts of Those You Love ... 131

Chapter 20: Planning Beyond Your Lifetime ... 132

96. Update Your Policies After Major Life Changes: Marriage, Divorce, Births, or Deaths ... 133

97. Designate Contingent Beneficiaries: Ensure Funds Are Distributed Even If Primary Beneficiaries Are Unavailable ... 134

98. Choose a Trusted Executor for Your Will and Policies: Avoid Family Conflict by Selecting Someone Impartial and Capable ... 135

99. Consider Legacy Planning With a Professional: Work With an Estate Planner or Financial Advisor to Maximize Your Impact ... 136

100. Leave Clear, Accessible Instructions for Your Plans: Make It Easy for Your Family to Carry Out Your Wishes ... 137

101. Trust in the Legacy You've Built: Know That Your Careful Planning Will Provide Love, Security, and Peace of Mind for Generations to Come ... 138

Conclusion: A Legacy Built on Love and Planning ... 139

Introduction

What does it mean to leave a legacy? For some, it's the inheritance they pass down—a house, savings, or treasured possessions. For others, it's the values and memories they leave behind, the stories that are told around family tables, and the traditions that carry on for generations. A true legacy, though, is more than just money or memories. It's the love, care, and thoughtful planning that ensure your family feels supported and connected long after you're gone.

"Your Legacy of Love: 101 Ways to Leave a Lasting Legacy" is a book born out of a desire to help people like you create a lasting impact. It's not just about financial security—although that's important. It's about crafting a legacy that speaks to who you are, what you value, and how deeply you care about your loved ones.

When we think of planning for the future, it's easy to feel overwhelmed. Words like "insurance," "trusts," and "estate planning" can seem distant and cold. But at its heart, legacy planning is an act of love. It's about showing your family that you cared enough to think ahead, to spare them unnecessary burdens, and to leave them with more than just assets—you're leaving them with peace of mind, emotional security, and a clear sense of your presence in their lives.

This book is your guide to doing just that. Together, we'll walk through 101 thoughtful, practical, and heartfelt ways to leave a legacy. We'll explore how to handle big-picture planning, like securing life insurance to protect your family financially or creating a will to ensure your wishes are honored. But we'll also dive into the deeply personal touches—writing letters for future milestones, recording your stories and wisdom, and establishing traditions that keep your memory alive.

You'll learn how to:

- Use life insurance to provide financial stability, pay off debts, and support your family's dreams.

- Create a funeral plan that reflects your values and spares your loved ones from difficult decisions.
- Establish scholarships, trusts, or charitable contributions to make a lasting impact in your community.
- Preserve your voice and values through videos, letters, and family rituals.
- Set up safeguards like trusts and financial advisors to ensure your family is guided and protected.

This book isn't just about preparing for the end of life—it's about making the most of the time you have right now. It's about living intentionally, celebrating milestones, and having open conversations with your loved ones. It's about recognizing that every step you take today is a step toward a future where your family feels your love and guidance, no matter what.

By the time you finish reading this book, you'll have the tools and inspiration to create a legacy that's uniquely yours—one that brings comfort, joy, and a deep sense of connection to the people who matter most to you. You'll know that your plans are in place, your love is felt, and your life has made a lasting difference.

This journey isn't about perfection; it's about care. And as you read, I hope you'll feel not just prepared, but also inspired—because the legacy you're building is one of the greatest gifts you can give. Let's begin this meaningful journey together.

Chapter 1: Emotional Gifts for Your Family

Imagine this: decades from now, your family is gathered around a table, flipping through letters, listening to voice recordings, or watching videos of you sharing your life, your thoughts, and your love. Someone might hold a carefully written letter in their hands, reading your words that speak directly to their heart, while another listens to your voice telling them, "I believe in you, and I'm so proud of who you've become." These are emotional gifts, the treasures that transcend time and create bonds that last forever.

Emotional gifts are the most profound and lasting inheritance you can give your family. Unlike material possessions, these gifts carry the essence of who you are—the love, wisdom, and experiences that define your connection with them. They aren't just keepsakes; they are timeless bridges of love and understanding that your family will return to in moments of joy, sorrow, or reflection.

Think about the emotions you want your family to feel when they think of you. Do you want them to feel loved, guided, and comforted, even when you're not physically present? Emotional gifts are your way of saying, "I was here, I loved you, and I'll always be a part of your life." They are your opportunity to leave a legacy that goes beyond the material, one that touches hearts and shapes futures.

The Power of Words

Writing a heartfelt letter is one of the simplest yet most impactful emotional gifts you can give. Take a moment to put pen to paper and share your feelings, memories, and hopes for the future. Write to your children, your spouse, your siblings, or even your closest friends. Tell them about the moments that made you proud, the lessons you've learned, and the dreams you have for them.

Imagine the joy your child will feel years later, reading a letter where you tell them, "I see your kindness, your courage, and your unique spark. Never doubt your ability to achieve *great things."* Those words will become their anchor, a source of comfort and encouragement in times of doubt.

The Gift of Presence

Recording your voice or creating a video message is another powerful way to connect with your family on a deep emotional level. Your voice has the ability to soothe, inspire, and remind your loved ones of your unwavering support. Create a recording where you share your life story, the values that guide you, or simply express your love and pride.

Picture your family, years from now, playing your video during a holiday gathering. They hear your laughter, see your smile, and feel your love as if you're right there with them. It's not just a recording; it's a moment of connection that spans time.

Traditions That Build Bonds

Emotional gifts aren't limited to physical or recorded items. Traditions can be just as powerful. Establish a weekly family dinner, an annual trip, or a special ritual that brings everyone together. These traditions create shared experiences and memories that your family will carry forward.

For example, you might decide to start a tradition of writing gratitude letters to each other every Thanksgiving or organizing a family storytelling night once a month. These moments of connection become the glue that holds families together, even when life pulls them in different directions.

A Legacy of Values

Your emotional gifts can also serve as a way to pass on your values and life lessons. Share the principles that guide you—integrity, compassion, perseverance—and illustrate them with stories from your own life. When your family reflects on these lessons, they'll find wisdom to navigate their own challenges.

For instance, if you've faced adversity and emerged stronger, share that journey. Let your family know how you overcame obstacles, what kept you motivated, and the lessons you learned along the way. Your experiences will become their roadmap, guiding them through life's twists and turns.

How Emotional Gifts Transform Both the Giver and the Receiver

Creating emotional gifts doesn't just benefit your family; it profoundly impacts you as well. Reflecting on your life, your relationships, and your values allows you to connect with what truly matters. It's a process of self-discovery and gratitude, giving you a sense of purpose and fulfillment.

When you create these gifts, you feel a deep connection to your loved ones. You'll experience the joy of knowing that you've expressed your love and left a part of yourself for them to cherish. It's a reminder that your presence, your love, and your wisdom will continue to shape their lives, even when you're not there to guide them directly.

Start Today

Don't wait for a "perfect" moment to begin. Write that letter, record that message, or start that tradition today. You don't need fancy tools or elaborate plans—what matters most is the authenticity and love behind your actions.

Remember, these emotional gifts are not just for your family; they're for you too. They allow you to reflect, connect, and find peace in the knowledge that your love and presence will always be with them.

What will your legacy be?

Will it be the things you owned, or the love you shared? The emotional gifts you create today will shape how your family remembers and feels connected to you forever. So, take the time to give them the greatest gift of all: *yourself*.

1. Write a Legacy Letter: Share Your Values, Dreams, and Wisdom

Explanation:
A legacy letter is a heartfelt written document where you express your values, beliefs, dreams, and advice to your loved ones. It's not a legal document but a personal message that communicates what truly matters to you. It's a way to ensure that your family and future generations understand the principles that guided your life.

Example:
In your letter, you might write about the importance of kindness and hard work, share your hopes for your grandchildren's futures, or offer wisdom from lessons you've learned.

Sample Excerpt:
"To my beloved family,
As I reflect on my life, I see how love, perseverance, and faith have been my guiding lights. Always remember that challenges are opportunities to grow. Dream big but cherish the small joys—like a sunrise, a kind word, or a good book. I hope you'll carry these values forward and build a life that makes you proud."

2. Record Personal Video Messages: Leave Heartfelt Words for Special Occasions

Explanation:
A video message allows you to leave a personal, emotional touch for your loved ones. These recordings can be tailored for specific milestones, such as birthdays, weddings, graduations, or even moments when encouragement might be needed.

Example:
Record a video for your child's wedding day, sharing your blessings and advice for a happy marriage. Or create a message congratulating a grandchild on their graduation and encouraging them to pursue their dreams.

Sample Script for a Wedding Video:
"Dear [Names],
Today is a momentous day in your lives, and though I may not be there in person, my heart is overflowing with love and joy for you both. Marriage is a partnership built on trust, laughter, and shared dreams. Cherish each other, forgive often, and always choose kindness. I'm so proud of you, and I know you'll create a beautiful life together."

3. Create a Family Photo Book: Highlight Cherished Memories and Milestones

Explanation:
A family photo book is a tangible collection of memories that captures the essence of your life and the lives of those you love. It serves as a visual story of your family's journey and provides an emotional connection for generations to come.

Example:
Include pictures of family vacations, significant milestones like anniversaries or birthdays, and candid moments that reflect the love and bond you share. Add captions or short stories to accompany each photo, explaining its significance.

Ideas for Sections:

- *"Our Beginnings"*: Photos of your childhood and early family history.
- *"Milestones"*: Key events like graduations, weddings, and births.
- *"Everyday Joys"*: Simple, candid moments like family dinners or holiday traditions.

Pro Tip: Consider creating a digital version for easy sharing and preserving.

4. Pass Down Meaningful Heirlooms: Attach Stories to Treasured Items

Explanation:
Family heirlooms are more than just objects—they carry stories and emotional value. By attaching a narrative to each heirloom, you ensure that its significance is understood and appreciated.

Example:
If you have your grandmother's quilt, share the story of how it was lovingly handmade and used during family gatherings. For a piece of jewelry, explain its history and why it symbolizes love or resilience in your family.

Sample Note for an Heirloom:
"This watch belonged to your grandfather, who wore it every day during his years working to support our family. It represents his dedication and love for us. I hope it inspires you to always work hard and cherish those you love."

5. Share Lessons Learned from Your Life Journey: Help Guide Future Generations

Explanation:
Life is a series of lessons, and your experiences can provide valuable guidance for your family. Sharing these lessons helps younger generations avoid pitfalls, appreciate life's blessings, and navigate challenges with wisdom.

Example:
You might share how you overcame financial struggles by budgeting and working hard or how you found joy in simple pleasures like gardening or cooking. Your stories can also highlight values such as integrity, resilience, and gratitude.

Sample Life Lesson:
"When I was in my 30s, I faced a time of financial hardship. It taught me the value of saving and living within my means. But it also showed me that true wealth lies in relationships and health. Remember, money can buy comfort, but love and purpose bring happiness."

Chapter 2: Life Insurance—Your Legacy's Cornerstone

Life insurance isn't just about money—it's about creating security for your loved ones and ensuring they're cared for, no matter what. It's a simple, powerful way to say, *"I've got your back, always."*

Why It Matters

Life insurance provides peace of mind. It covers the mortgage, daily expenses, or college tuition, giving your family the space to grieve without financial stress. It's a lifeline that supports their future and keeps your love alive.

A Lasting Legacy

Beyond covering costs, life insurance allows you to leave a legacy—helping your family thrive, funding dreams, or supporting causes that matter to you. It's a way to make your presence felt, even when you're not there.

Take Action Today

From term policies for short-term needs to whole life coverage for lasting security, life insurance is an investment in your family's future. Start planning now—it's the ultimate gift of love.

6. Purchase a Life Insurance Policy: Ensure Your Loved Ones Have Financial Stability

Explanation:
Life insurance provides a financial safety net for your family when you're no longer there to support them. It can cover essential expenses like housing, daily living costs, or debts, ensuring your loved ones can maintain their quality of life.

Example:
If you're the primary earner in the family, purchasing a life insurance policy for $500,000 might provide enough for your spouse to pay off the mortgage, cover annual expenses, and support your children's education.

Tip:
Work with a licensed insurance agent to assess your needs and identify the best policy for your situation.

7. Choose the Right Coverage Amount: Calculate Your Family's Future Needs

Explanation:

The amount of life insurance coverage you purchase should be based on your family's projected financial needs. This includes paying off debts, funding education, and maintaining household income.

Example Calculation:

- Outstanding Mortgage: $200,000
- Children's College Tuition: $150,000
- Living Expenses for 10 Years: $300,000
- Final Expenses (Adjusted for Inflation): $30,000

Total Coverage Need: $680,000

You might round this amount to $700,000 to account for unexpected costs or higher inflation rates. This ensures your family has the resources they need.

Tip:

Use an online life insurance calculator or consult with an insurance professional for a personalized assessment.

8. Understand Term vs. Whole Life Insurance: Choose What Aligns with Your Long-Term Goals

Explanation:
The type of life insurance you choose impacts your coverage and financial planning.

- **Term Life Insurance:** Provides coverage for a specific period (e.g., 10, 20, or 30 years) and is generally more affordable. It's ideal for covering temporary needs like a mortgage or child-rearing costs.
- **Whole Life Insurance:** Offers lifelong coverage with an investment component, allowing you to build cash value over time. It's more expensive but can serve as a tool for estate planning.

Example:
- A 30-year-old parent might choose a $1 million, 20-year term policy to cover expenses until their children are independent.
- A retiree might choose a smaller whole life policy to ensure funds for final expenses and leave a legacy.

Tip:
Evaluate your budget and goals before deciding which type works best for you.

9. Add a Final Expense Policy: Cover Funeral Costs and Eliminate Financial Stress for Your Family

Explanation:
Final expense insurance is a smaller policy designed specifically to cover funeral and burial or cremation costs. These costs are projected to rise significantly due to inflation over the next 15-20 years.

Example with Adjusted Costs:
The **current average funeral cost** (including burial, casket, and services) is approximately $10,000-$12,000. With an inflation rate of 3% annually over 20 years, this could rise to **$18,000-$20,000**. Cremation, currently costing around $6,000, could rise to **$10,000-$12,000** in the same timeframe.

Purchasing a $25,000 final expense policy ensures your loved ones have ample funds for:

- Funeral or cremation costs.
- Memorial services and flowers.
- Travel expenses for family members to attend.

Tip:
Final expense policies are often easier to qualify for and provide peace of mind that these costs won't burden your family.

10. Review Your Policy Regularly: Ensure It Reflects Any Life Changes

Explanation:
Life changes, such as marriage, the birth of a child, or retirement, can significantly affect your insurance needs. Reviewing your policy ensures it aligns with your current situation and goals.

Examples of Life Changes Requiring Updates:

- **Marriage:** Add your spouse as a beneficiary.
- **Children:** Increase your coverage to account for future educational costs.
- **Retirement:** Adjust your policy if your debts are paid off and your children are financially independent.
- **Divorce:** Remove a former spouse as a beneficiary.

Tip:
Set a reminder to review your policy every 2-3 years or after any major life event.

Chapter 3: Planning for Final Expenses

Let's talk about something that's not easy but incredibly important: planning for final expenses. While it's a tough topic, taking the time to plan is one of the most loving gifts you can give your family. Instead of leaving them overwhelmed by financial stress or uncertain about your wishes, you give them the freedom to grieve, celebrate your life, and support one another.

Why Plan?

Final expenses like funerals, medical bills, and outstanding debts add up quickly, often reaching $7,000 to $12,000 or more. Planning ahead ensures these costs are covered and sends a clear message to your loved ones: *"I care about you enough to handle this."*

Simple Ways to Prepare

- Life Insurance: Earmark funds specifically for final expenses.
- Prepaid Plans: Lock in today's prices for funeral services.
- Dedicated Savings: Create an accessible account for these costs.
- Final Expense Insurance: A small, focused policy for burial or memorial expenses.

The Gift of Peace

Imagine your family, stress-free, focused on celebrating your life and supporting each other, instead of scrambling for answers or funds. Planning ahead gives them clarity and peace during a difficult time.

Take the First Step

Start by writing down your wishes, discussing them with your loved ones, and documenting everything. It's a small effort now for a lasting impact later.

A Legacy of Love

This isn't just about finances—it's about leaving behind comfort, care, and love. By planning your final expenses, you ensure your family feels supported and secure, even in your absence.

11. Prepay Funeral Expenses: Lock in Costs and Ease Financial Pressure on Loved Ones

Explanation:
Prepaying funeral expenses can secure today's prices for services, burial plots, or cremation. This can help reduce future costs caused by inflation and relieve your family from financial burdens during a difficult time.

Example:

- Prepay $15,000 for a funeral service that includes a burial plot, casket, and ceremony, ensuring your family won't have to cover the costs later.

Benefits:

- Guarantees the funds are used specifically for your funeral preferences.
- Protects against future price increases.

Pitfalls to Avoid:

- Limited Portability: Some prepayment plans are tied to specific funeral homes, making them less useful if you relocate.
- Risk of Business Closure: If the funeral home goes out of business, your prepaid funds could be at risk.
- Inflation Coverage: Some plans may not fully account for inflation over time.

Tip:
Review the plan's terms carefully to ensure it's transferable and includes inflation adjustments.

12. Create a Funeral Plan: Document Your Wishes for Services, Burial, or Cremation

Explanation:
A funeral plan outlines your specific preferences for your final arrangements, reducing uncertainty and ensuring your wishes are respected. This can include details about the type of service, burial or cremation, and personal touches.

Example:

- Service Type: Memorial at a favorite location with music and a eulogy from a close friend.
- Disposition: Cremation, with ashes scattered at a meaningful place.
- Personal Details: Your favorite flowers, songs, and photos to be displayed.

Benefits:

- Provides clear guidance for your family, preventing disagreements or guesswork.
- Ensures your service reflects your personality and values.

Tip:
Store your funeral plan with your will or in a legacy binder, and share it with your executor or family members.

13. Research Funeral Insurance: A Dedicated Policy Ensures All Final Costs Are Covered

Explanation:

Funeral insurance, also known as final expense insurance, is a small whole life policy specifically designed to cover end-of-life expenses. It can provide financial relief without tying you to a specific funeral home.

Example:

- Purchase a $20,000 funeral insurance policy to cover the cost of services, burial or cremation, and other related expenses.

Benefits:

- Funds are accessible to your family immediately upon your passing.
- Offers flexibility for your family to use the funds as needed.

Tip:

Compare policies from reputable insurers and ensure the coverage amount accounts for inflation.

14. Choose a Trusted Beneficiary: Select Someone Responsible to Manage Final Arrangements

Explanation:
Your beneficiary is responsible for receiving life insurance or funeral insurance proceeds and managing your final arrangements. Selecting someone dependable ensures your funds are used as intended.

Example:

- Name your spouse or adult child as your primary beneficiary. Designate a backup (contingent beneficiary) in case the primary is unable to fulfill the role.

Benefits:

- Ensures your arrangements are handled responsibly and according to your wishes.
- Reduces the likelihood of delays or mismanagement.

Tip:
Communicate your plans clearly with your chosen beneficiary and provide them with access to relevant documents.

15. Include Obituary Funds in Your Plan: Cover the Cost of a Meaningful Memorial Announcement

Explanation:
Obituaries honor your life and inform others of your passing and service details. Including funds in your plan ensures this tribute is both meaningful and properly funded.

Example:
- Allocate $1,000 to $2,000 in your funeral insurance or savings to cover the cost of publishing obituaries in newspapers or online platforms.

Benefits:
- Ensures your obituary reflects your achievements and values.
- Provides a way for distant friends and family to stay informed.

Tip:
Draft a preliminary obituary yourself or provide key details for your family to include, such as career highlights, hobbies, and personal anecdotes.

Chapter 4: Financial Stability for Loved Ones

Financial stability is one of the greatest gifts you can give your family. It's not just about money—it's about creating security, peace, and opportunity for the people you care about most. Imagine your loved ones free from financial stress, able to pursue dreams and build meaningful lives, all because of the foundation you've created.

Why it Matters: Without financial stability, uncertainty can create tension and limit opportunities. But with intentional planning, you provide your family the freedom to thrive. Savings, paying off debt, and securing insurance are small steps that lead to a big impact.

Real-Life Impact: Picture your loved ones focusing on their future, not worrying about bills or debts. Your planning creates peace of mind and opens doors to education, growth, and stronger relationships.

Start today. Each step—saving, budgeting, or creating a will—brings you closer to a legacy of love and security. Financial stability isn't just numbers; it's the gift of a better, brighter future for those you hold dear.

16. Create a Financial Blueprint for Your Family: Outline Your Current and Future Assets

Explanation:
A financial blueprint is a comprehensive overview of your assets, liabilities, income, and expenses. It helps your family understand your financial situation and makes it easier to manage or distribute assets after your passing.

Example:

- **Current Assets**: Home equity, savings accounts, retirement funds, investments.
- **Liabilities**: Mortgage balance, credit card debt, car loans.
- **Future Assets**: Life insurance payouts, pensions, annuities.
- **Ongoing Expenses**: Monthly bills, insurance premiums, and planned contributions (e.g., education funds).

Tip:
Include clear instructions on accessing accounts, policies, and important documents. Use a "Legacy Binder" or digital organizer to consolidate everything in one place.

17. Use Life Insurance to Pay Off Debts: Avoid Leaving Unpaid Loans or Credit Card Balances

Explanation:
Life insurance can be used to clear outstanding debts, ensuring your loved ones aren't burdened with financial obligations. This includes mortgages, car loans, medical bills, and credit card balances.

Example:
If you have a $200,000 mortgage and $15,000 in credit card debt, ensure your life insurance policy covers at least $250,000 (including a buffer for interest or inflation). This allows your family to live debt-free after your passing.

Tip:
Update your beneficiary regularly to reflect your current family situation and confirm they understand the intended purpose of the funds.

18. Set Up an Education Fund: Provide for Children or Grandchildren's College Expenses

Explanation:

An education fund ensures your children or grandchildren have access to resources for their future learning. Life insurance benefits can be allocated to such funds, or you can establish dedicated accounts like 529 plans.

Example:

Set aside $50,000 from a life insurance policy for a grandchild's college expenses. Alternatively, open a 529 plan and fund it incrementally during your lifetime, with life insurance providing additional coverage.

Tip:

Communicate your intentions with the fund's beneficiaries and consider setting guidelines for how the money should be used (e.g., tuition, books, or educational travel).

19. Consider a Joint Life Insurance Policy: Cover Both You and Your Spouse Under One Plan

Explanation:
A joint life insurance policy insures two people—typically spouses—and pays out upon the first or second death, depending on the policy type. It can be more cost-effective than purchasing two separate policies.

Example:
A couple in their 50s could purchase a $500,000 joint life policy that pays out after one partner passes. This can cover funeral expenses, debts, and provide the surviving spouse with financial stability.

Tip:
Evaluate whether a "first-to-die" or "second-to-die" policy fits your family's needs:

- **First-to-die**: Pays out immediately after one spouse's death.
- **Second-to-die**: Delays payout until both spouses have passed, ideal for estate planning.

20. Ensure Coverage for Long-Term Care: Life Insurance Riders Can Help with Medical or Elder Care Costs

Explanation:
Long-term care (LTC) riders on life insurance policies provide funds to cover expenses like assisted living, nursing homes, or in-home care. These costs can be significant, and having a policy with an LTC rider helps protect your assets.

Example:
If you develop a chronic condition requiring $100,000 in long-term care, an LTC rider allows you to access a portion of your life insurance benefits while still alive to cover these costs.

Tip:
Compare policies to find one with flexible and affordable LTC rider options. Ensure the coverage amount accounts for inflation in healthcare costs over the next 15-20 years.

Chapter 5: Estate Planning Made Simple

Estate planning is a profound act of love and responsibility. It's about more than just financial or legal arrangements—it's a way to ensure your family feels supported and cared for during a challenging time. By thoughtfully planning, you ease their emotional and logistical burdens, allowing them to focus on healing and cherishing your memory.

Without a plan, families often face legal complications, financial stress, and tough decisions. However, a clear estate plan provides a roadmap for your wishes. Whether it's a will to distribute assets, naming beneficiaries, or creating directives for healthcare, every step ensures your intentions are honored and your loved ones are protected.

Estate planning is a thoughtful act of love that ensures your family's clarity and peace of mind. Start with simple steps like drafting a will, naming beneficiaries, and organizing key documents. It's not about wealth, but about showing care and creating a legacy of love that comforts your family even in your absence.

21. Write a Comprehensive Will: Outline Your Wishes for Property and Assets

Explanation:

A will is a legal document that specifies how your property and assets should be distributed after your death. Without a will, state laws may determine the division of your estate, which might not align with your wishes. A comprehensive will also designate guardians for minor children and appoint an executor to carry out your plans.

Example:

- **Property Distribution**: Leave your house to your eldest child and divide your savings equally among your children.
- **Sentimental Items**: Bequeath your grandmother's ring to your granddaughter and your tools to your son who loves woodworking.
- **Charitable Contributions**: Donate a portion of your estate to a local animal shelter.

Tip:

Consult with an estate attorney to ensure your will is legally binding and complete.

22. Establish a Living Trust: Protect Your Assets and Avoid Probate

Explanation:
A living trust is a legal arrangement where your assets are placed under the management of a trustee for your benefit during your lifetime and then passed to your beneficiaries upon your death. It bypasses the probate process, saving time and legal expenses, while also keeping your financial matters private.

Example:
Transfer ownership of your home, investment accounts, and other significant assets to a living trust. Appoint yourself as the trustee to retain control during your life and name a successor trustee to manage or distribute assets after your passing.

Tip:
A revocable living trust can be adjusted as your financial situation or family circumstances change.

23. Update Your Life Insurance Beneficiaries: Ensure They Reflect Your Current Relationships

Explanation:
Life insurance benefits are distributed directly to the named beneficiaries, overriding what is stated in your will. Regularly updating your beneficiary designations ensures they reflect your current relationships and intentions.

Example:

- **Marriage:** Add your spouse as the primary beneficiary.
- **Children:** Add a new child or grandchild to the policy.
- **Divorce:** Remove a former spouse if applicable.

Tip:
Periodically review all beneficiary designations across life insurance policies, retirement accounts, and investment plans to avoid conflicts or unintended consequences.

---

24. Name a Power of Attorney: Choose Someone to Handle Finances if You Become Incapacitated

Explanation:
A power of attorney (POA) grants a trusted individual the authority to make financial decisions and manage your affairs if you're unable to do so. This can include paying bills, managing investments, or selling property.

Example:
Appoint your spouse or a financially responsible adult child as your durable POA. For instance, they could access your accounts to pay for medical expenses or manage rental property income during your incapacity.

Tip:
Work with a legal professional to create a durable power of attorney document that remains valid even if you lose mental capacity.

25. Document Your Digital Assets: Include Passwords and Online Account Details for Easy Access

Explanation:
Your digital assets, such as online accounts, passwords, and digital subscriptions, need to be accessible to your executor or trusted family members. Documenting these details ensures a seamless transition in managing or closing these accounts.

Example:
- **Online Accounts**: Bank accounts, email accounts, and investment platforms.
- **Social Media**: Facebook, Instagram, and LinkedIn profiles for memorialization or closure.
- **Subscriptions**: Netflix, Spotify, and cloud storage services.

Tip:
Use a password manager to securely store login details and share access with your executor. Include instructions for accessing digital wallets, cryptocurrency, or any other digital financial accounts.

Chapter 6: Protecting Your Legacy with Insurance: A Blueprint for Peace of Mind

Insurance is more than a policy—it's a *promise* of enduring love and stability for your family's future. Think of it as a financial safety net that ensures your loved ones can thrive, even when life takes unexpected turns. Life insurance becomes a *lifeline*, covering essential expenses; health insurance acts as a shield against staggering medical bills, and long-term care insurance safeguards your hard-earned savings in your golden years. These aren't just financial tools—they're the *anchors* of a well-planned legacy.

Picture this: Your family navigating life with confidence because you took the time to plan. A mother's life insurance funds her children's dreams of college; a grandfather's long-term care insurance preserves his dignity and financial security. These aren't just numbers or policies—they're *acts of love* that ensure your family's freedom to grieve, heal, and move forward with peace of mind.

By taking these intentional steps, you're doing more than protecting your family's future—you're creating a *roadmap of care* that ensures your memory is felt in every decision they make. This is your opportunity to leave behind not just wealth but *a lasting impact of love and foresight*.

26. Invest in Permanent Life Insurance: Build Cash Value While Securing Future Benefits

Explanation:
Permanent life insurance, such as whole life or universal life, provides lifelong coverage while building cash value over time. The cash value grows tax-deferred and can be accessed during your lifetime for expenses like education, emergencies, or retirement.

Example:
A $250,000 whole life insurance policy for a 40-year-old can accumulate cash value over the years, allowing the policyholder to borrow against it or withdraw funds while maintaining the death benefit.

Benefits:
- Lifelong coverage without the need to renew.
- A source of liquid assets you can access for personal or financial needs.
- A guaranteed payout to beneficiaries regardless of when you pass.

Tip:
Permanent life insurance is more expensive than term life but offers additional benefits. Evaluate your long-term needs and budget before investing.

27. Consider Burial Insurance: Specifically Designed to Cover End-of-Life Expenses

Explanation:
Burial insurance, also called final expense insurance, is a small whole life policy designed to cover funeral and burial costs. It ensures your family isn't left struggling to pay for your final arrangements.

Example:
A $15,000 burial insurance policy can cover inflation-adjusted funeral expenses, including services, burial or cremation, and related costs such as flowers and transportation.

Benefits:

- Easy to qualify for, even with health issues.
- Affordable premiums tailored for older individuals.
- Funds are available quickly, allowing your family to handle expenses without delay.

Pitfalls to Avoid:

- Ensure the coverage amount is adequate for future inflation.
- Avoid policies with excessive fees or unclear terms.

28. Explore Accidental Death Policies: Add Extra Protection for Unforeseen Events

Explanation:
Accidental death and dismemberment (AD&D) policies provide additional coverage if you pass away or suffer severe injury due to an accident. This type of policy supplements your primary life insurance and provides financial security in unexpected situations.

Example:
If you have a $500,000 AD&D policy and pass away in a car accident, your family could receive the additional payout on top of your regular life insurance benefit.

Benefits:

- Low-cost way to increase your coverage.
- Provides financial relief for accidents, which often involve unforeseen expenses.
- Includes partial payouts for injuries like loss of limbs or vision.

Tip:
AD&D policies are ideal for individuals in high-risk professions or those seeking additional coverage without increasing their primary life insurance.

29. Add Critical Illness Riders: Ensure Coverage if You Face Serious Health Challenges

Explanation:
A critical illness rider can be added to your life insurance policy, allowing you to access a portion of your death benefit if you're diagnosed with a severe illness, such as cancer, heart disease, or a stroke. This provides financial support during expensive medical treatments.

Example:
If you have a $500,000 policy with a critical illness rider, you might be able to access $100,000 to cover treatments or related expenses if you're diagnosed with a qualifying condition.

Benefits:

- Covers medical expenses not included in health insurance.
- Provides income replacement if you're unable to work.
- Offers peace of mind during a health crisis.

Tip:
Carefully review the conditions and payout structure of the rider. Not all illnesses or treatments may qualify for benefits.

30. Bundle Policies for Savings: Combine Life, Health, and Burial Insurance for Better Rates

Explanation:
Bundling multiple insurance policies with the same provider can lower premiums and simplify management. Many insurers offer discounts for customers who combine life, health, and burial insurance under one plan.

Example:
A provider might offer a 10% discount for bundling a $500,000 life insurance policy, a health insurance plan, and a $15,000 burial insurance policy.

Benefits:
- Cost savings through multi-policy discounts.
- Easier management with a single provider and billing process.
- Comprehensive coverage addressing multiple needs.

Pitfalls to Avoid:
- Ensure the bundled policies meet your specific needs; discounts shouldn't come at the expense of adequate coverage.
- Compare individual and bundled plans to confirm you're receiving genuine savings.

Tip:
Ask your insurance provider about bundling options and compare quotes from multiple companies to ensure you're getting the best deal.

Chapter 7: Securing a Debt-Free Future

Picture this: your loved ones, thriving, unburdened by financial strain, and living a life of opportunity because you took the steps to secure their future. That's the power of eliminating debt and ensuring a debt-free legacy. It's not just about numbers—it's about freedom, peace, and empowerment for generations to come.

Why Securing a Debt-Free Future Matters
Debt can weigh heavily on your family's future, limiting opportunities and creating stress. Leaving a debt-free legacy ensures your loved ones can move forward confidently without financial burdens holding them back.

The Freedom of Financial Stability
A debt-free future gives your family the gift of freedom—freedom to focus on their dreams and goals without the worry of unpaid bills. It's about providing peace of mind and a foundation for success.

Empower Your Family for the Future
Teaching financial literacy and building an emergency fund ensures your loved ones are prepared for life's challenges. A debt-free legacy isn't just about numbers; it's about leaving behind security, freedom, and hope.

31. Use Life Insurance to Cover Mortgages: Prevent Your Family From Losing Their Home

Explanation:
A life insurance policy can ensure your family has the funds to pay off a mortgage, relieving them of the financial stress of monthly payments. This guarantees they can keep their home after your passing.

Example:
If your mortgage balance is $250,000, you can purchase a life insurance policy for at least that amount. Upon your passing, the proceeds will allow your family to pay off the mortgage entirely.

Benefits:
- Ensures your family retains their home and stability.
- Removes one of the largest financial obligations for your heirs.

Tip:
Consider matching your policy's term length to the remaining years on your mortgage if using term life insurance.

32. Pay Off Car Loans With Insurance Proceeds: Remove Additional Burdens

Explanation:
Life insurance can also cover car loans, preventing repossession and ensuring your loved ones can maintain their mobility. This is particularly helpful if a vehicle is essential for work or daily activities.

Example:
If you owe $20,000 on a car loan, include this amount in your life insurance coverage calculation. This ensures your family can own the vehicle outright after your passing.

Benefits:
- Frees your family from monthly loan payments.
- Helps maintain their transportation needs without financial strain.

Tip:
Combine the outstanding balance of car loans with other debts when determining your total insurance coverage needs.

33. Eliminate Lingering Medical Bills: Ensure No Debts Remain Unpaid

Explanation:
If you incur significant medical expenses before passing, these debts could fall to your estate or family members. Life insurance proceeds can ensure all outstanding medical bills are paid, protecting your loved ones from unexpected financial obligations.

Example:
If your medical expenses total $50,000, life insurance benefits can cover this amount so that your family isn't left with debt collectors.

Benefits:
- Clears financial liabilities tied to your healthcare.
- Prevents creditors from seizing estate assets to cover medical costs.

Tip:
Factor in potential future healthcare costs when calculating your insurance needs, especially if you have a chronic illness or foresee extended care.

34. Provide for Final Utility and Tax Payments: Avoid Unexpected Costs for Your Heirs

Explanation:
Utility bills, property taxes, and other recurring expenses don't disappear after your passing. Life insurance proceeds can cover these final payments, ensuring your heirs don't face sudden, unexpected costs.

Example:
Allocate $5,000-$10,000 from your life insurance benefits to cover final utility bills, property taxes, and homeowner association fees until your estate is settled.

Benefits:
- Prevents utility shut-offs or late fees on tax payments.
- Keeps property in good standing while your estate is being distributed.

Tip:
Work with an estate planner to estimate these final costs and include them in your insurance coverage.

35. Include Funds for Estate Taxes: Large Estates May Require Additional Coverage

Explanation:
If your estate exceeds the federal or state estate tax exemption limits, your heirs may be required to pay significant taxes. Life insurance can provide the liquidity needed to cover these taxes without forcing the sale of assets.

Example:
If your estate is valued at $15 million and the federal estate tax exemption is $13 million, the taxable amount would be $2 million. Allocate sufficient life insurance benefits to cover the estate tax on this amount (up to 40%, or $800,000).

Benefits:
- Prevents the need to liquidate family assets or businesses.
- Ensures your estate plan is carried out as intended.

Tip:
Consult with an estate planning attorney or financial advisor to determine the exact amount of additional coverage needed for estate taxes.

Chapter 8: Supporting End-of-Life Decisions

End-of-Life Planning: A Gift of Love
Planning for end-of-life decisions may feel heavy, but it's one of the most caring acts you can do for your family. By addressing these choices now, you ease their burden, providing clarity and comfort during difficult times.

Why It Matters
Without a plan, families face tough decisions in moments of grief. Clear instructions on medical care, funeral preferences, and financial arrangements ensure they can focus on celebrating your life, not navigating uncertainty.

Getting Started
Define your priorities, document your wishes, and share them with loved ones. Tools like living wills, life insurance, and prepaid plans protect your family emotionally and financially.

A Legacy of Peace
End-of-life planning isn't about fear—it's about love. It gives your family the gift of clarity and the confidence that they're honoring your wishes, creating a legacy of care and stability.

36. Create an Advance Directive: Outline Your Medical Care Preferences

Explanation:
An advance directive, also known as a living will, is a legal document that specifies your medical care preferences in case you become unable to communicate. It covers decisions such as life support, resuscitation, and pain management.

Example:
- Specify whether you want life-prolonging treatments like mechanical ventilation or feeding tubes.
- Indicate your preference for pain relief even if it may shorten your life.

Benefits:
- Ensures your healthcare choices align with your values.
- Reduces emotional stress on your family by guiding their decisions.

Tip:
Work with an attorney or use state-specific templates to ensure your advance directive is legally binding and properly filed.

37. Discuss Your Wishes With Loved Ones: Avoid Misunderstandings During Difficult Times

Explanation:
Having open conversations with your family about your medical and end-of-life preferences ensures they understand your wishes. This prevents confusion or conflict during critical moments.

Example:
Share your preferences for:

- End-of-life care (e.g., hospice or home care).
- Burial or cremation.
- Organ donation.

Benefits:

- Promotes transparency and reduces emotional conflict among family members.
- Ensures your wishes are respected even if they aren't explicitly written down.

Tip:
Schedule a family meeting or one-on-one conversations to share your plans. Use this time to answer questions and address concerns.

38. Appoint a Healthcare Proxy: Select Someone You Trust to Make Medical Decisions

Explanation:
A healthcare proxy, or medical power of attorney, is a person you authorize to make medical decisions on your behalf if you're unable to do so. This individual should understand your values and be willing to advocate for your wishes.

Example:
Appoint your spouse, adult child, or a trusted friend who:

- Understands your preferences for life support and treatments.
- Can handle stressful situations and communicate effectively with healthcare providers.

Benefits:

- Ensures someone you trust is making decisions for you.
- Provides clarity and authority in medical emergencies.

Tip:
Discuss your wishes with your proxy in detail and provide them with a copy of your advance directive.

39. Include End-of-Life Care in Your Insurance Plan: Consider Policies That Cover Hospice and Palliative Care

Explanation:
Hospice and palliative care focus on comfort and quality of life during the final stages of illness. Some insurance policies offer riders or standalone plans to cover these services, reducing financial strain on your family.

Example:
If you require hospice care, which can cost $5,000-$7,000 per month, an insurance policy with an end-of-life care rider can cover these expenses.

Benefits:

- Provides funding for compassionate care in a preferred setting, such as your home or a hospice facility.
- Eases the financial burden on your family while ensuring comfort and dignity.

Tip:
When choosing an insurance policy, inquire about hospice and palliative care benefits. If your current policy lacks coverage, consider adding a rider or supplemental insurance.

40. Document Burial or Cremation Preferences: Provide Clarity and Peace of Mind

Explanation:
Documenting your burial or cremation preferences ensures your family knows your wishes, avoiding potential conflicts or guesswork. Include details such as the type of service, location, and any personal touches.

Example:
- **Burial:** Specify the cemetery and plot, type of casket, and desired headstone inscription.
- **Cremation:** Outline whether your ashes should be kept, scattered, or interred.

Benefits:
- Prevents family disagreements about how to honor your memory.
- Ensures your final arrangements reflect your values and desires.

Tip:
Include this information in your funeral plan and share it with your healthcare proxy or executor to ensure it is accessible when needed.

Chapter 9: Leveraging Life Insurance for Legacy Projects

Imagine Leaving a Lasting Legacy

What if your life's work and values could continue shaping the world even after you're gone? Life insurance isn't just a financial tool—it's a gateway to funding your passions and creating a legacy that inspires.

Why Life Insurance for Legacy Projects?

Life insurance offers tax-free benefits and flexibility, making it an ideal way to fund your legacy. By naming beneficiaries like charities or family trusts, your policy ensures your impact continues without delays or taxes diminishing your gift.

Steps to Build Your Legacy

Start by defining what matters most—be it education, philanthropy, or family stability. Choose beneficiaries, consult a financial advisor, and customize your policy with riders that suit your goals.

A Legacy That Inspires

Leaving a legacy isn't just financial—it's emotional. Knowing your policy will fund meaningful projects brings peace of mind and demonstrates purpose-driven planning to loved ones. Let life insurance become the cornerstone of a story that echoes your values, dreams, and lasting impact for generations to come.

41. Fund Scholarships or Education Trusts: Create Opportunities for Future Generations

Explanation:
Setting up a scholarship or education trust ensures that your values of education and growth live on. These funds can help children, grandchildren, or even community members access educational opportunities they might not otherwise afford.

Example:
- Create a $50,000 education trust for your grandchildren, ensuring they have funds for tuition and books.
- Establish a community scholarship in your name for local high school students pursuing college or trade school.

Benefits:
- Provides a lasting legacy tied to learning and personal growth.
- Empowers future generations to achieve their potential.

Tip:
Work with a financial advisor or legal expert to set up the trust or scholarship, ensuring it aligns with your goals and provides clear guidelines for use.

42. Support Charitable Causes: Name a Nonprofit as a Beneficiary

Explanation:
Naming a nonprofit organization as a beneficiary in your will or life insurance policy is a powerful way to give back to causes you're passionate about. This ensures your values continue to make an impact even after your passing.

Example:
- Designate 10% of your life insurance benefits to a charity supporting education, healthcare, or environmental conservation.
- Include a nonprofit in your estate plan, such as your local animal shelter or a global humanitarian organization.

Benefits:
- Leaves a lasting mark on the world by contributing to meaningful causes.
- May provide tax benefits to your estate, reducing liabilities for your heirs.

Tip:
Contact the charity to confirm their beneficiary designation process and discuss how your gift can best be utilized.

43. Provide a Financial Cushion for Your Spouse: Ensure They Can Live Comfortably After Your Passing

Explanation:
Life insurance proceeds can help your spouse maintain their lifestyle, cover daily expenses, and plan for the future. This is particularly important if they rely on your income or face unexpected costs after your passing.

Example:
- Purchase a $500,000 life insurance policy to cover living expenses, healthcare, and future travel for your spouse.
- Use permanent life insurance to build cash value, which your spouse can access during retirement.

Benefits:
- Eases the transition after your passing by removing financial stress.
- Ensures your spouse has the resources to age comfortably and independently.

Tip:
Factor in inflation and potential long-term care needs when calculating the financial cushion required.

44. Help Your Children or Grandchildren Buy Homes: Allocate Part of Your Insurance Benefits for Housing

Explanation:
Homeownership is a significant milestone that can provide stability and generational wealth. Allocating part of your life insurance benefits to help with a down payment or mortgage can make this dream achievable for your loved ones.

Example:
- Specify $50,000 from your life insurance policy to assist each child or grandchild with a down payment on their first home.
- Set up a trust with clear guidelines for when and how funds can be accessed for housing.

Benefits:
- Provides tangible, long-term support for your family's financial well-being.
- Helps create a sense of security and belonging through homeownership.

Tip:
Discuss your intentions with your beneficiaries to ensure they understand the purpose and conditions of the funds.

45. Leave a Lasting Family Fund: Establish a Resource for Emergencies or Celebrations

Explanation:
A family fund is a flexible financial resource that can be used for various purposes, such as medical emergencies, weddings, or family reunions. It serves as a safety net and a celebration fund, keeping your family connected and supported.

Example:
- Allocate $100,000 from your estate to a family trust fund, managed by a trusted family member or financial advisor.
- Specify that the fund can be used for medical emergencies, milestone celebrations, or supporting family members in need.

Benefits:
- Strengthens family bonds by creating a shared resource.
- Provides financial stability and reduces stress during unexpected situations.

Tip:
Set clear rules for accessing the fund to ensure it's used fairly and responsibly by all family members.

Chapter 10: Practical Planning for Loved Ones

Practical Planning: A Gift of Love and Security
Preparing for your family's future is one of the most meaningful ways to show your care. Practical planning ensures your loved ones feel supported, guided, and secure during life's most difficult moments. It's not just about finances—it's about leaving a legacy of clarity and love.

Why Planning Matters
Imagine your family facing emotional stress and financial uncertainty without guidance. By planning now, you give them the gift of *peace of mind* and a clear path forward. It's a way to protect them from unnecessary burdens while reflecting your thoughtfulness and care.

Steps to Start Today
Begin with simple actions: document your wishes in a will or healthcare directive, organize important documents in one secure location, and communicate your plans with your family to ensure everyone understands your intentions.

A Legacy of Love
Practical planning is more than logistics—it's an emotional gift. By taking steps today, you ensure your family feels your love and guidance even in your absence. Give them the priceless gift of security, clarity, and lasting peace.

46. Leave Clear Instructions for Accessing Insurance Benefits: Help Beneficiaries File Claims Easily

Explanation:
Filing insurance claims during an emotional time can be overwhelming for beneficiaries. By providing clear instructions, you simplify the process and ensure your loved ones can access the benefits without delays.

Example:
- Write a step-by-step guide for each life insurance policy, including contact information for the insurance company, policy numbers, and required documents (e.g., death certificate).
- Include a list of any other benefits tied to your employer or government programs.

Benefits:
- Speeds up the payout process.
- Reduces stress and confusion for beneficiaries.

Tip:
Review the claims process with your family in advance and provide a trusted family member or advisor with a copy of the instructions.

47. Compile a "Legacy Binder": Include Policies, Accounts, and Instructions

Explanation:
A legacy binder is a centralized collection of documents that includes all essential financial, legal, and personal information. It serves as a one-stop resource for your beneficiaries to manage your affairs after your passing.

Example:
Your binder could include:

- Life insurance policies and contact information.
- Wills, trusts, and advance directives.
- Bank account details and investment portfolios.
- Digital asset information (e.g., passwords).

Benefits:

- Reduces the chance of missed or overlooked accounts and assets.
- Makes it easier for your executor or beneficiaries to handle your estate efficiently.

Tip:
Keep your binder updated and store it in a secure, fireproof location. Inform a trusted family member or advisor where it can be found.

48. Educate Your Family on Financial Literacy: Empower Them to Manage Your Gifts Wisely

Explanation:
Financial literacy equips your family with the skills to manage the inheritance or insurance benefits you leave behind. Without this knowledge, they may struggle with budgeting, investing, or avoiding scams.

Example:
- Host family meetings to discuss basic financial principles, such as saving, investing, and debt management.
- Recommend resources, such as books or online courses, to help them grow their financial knowledge.

Benefits:
- Increases the likelihood that your legacy will be preserved and used effectively.
- Reduces the risk of poor financial decisions or mismanagement.

Tip:
Consider working with a financial advisor to provide personalized guidance for your beneficiaries.

49. Create an Emergency Fund Through Insurance Savings: Prepare for Unexpected Needs

Explanation:
An emergency fund ensures your family has a financial safety net to cover unexpected expenses, such as medical emergencies, car repairs, or sudden job loss. Life insurance proceeds can be allocated to establish or bolster this fund.

Example:
Set aside $50,000 from your life insurance benefits in a high-yield savings account for your spouse or children to use during financial crises.

Benefits:
- Provides immediate financial relief in emergencies.
- Reduces stress during uncertain times.

Tip:
Designate a trusted family member to oversee the emergency fund and ensure it's used only for its intended purpose.

50. Assign a Trusted Advisor: Guide Your Family Through Financial and Legal Processes

Explanation:
A trusted advisor, such as a financial planner, estate attorney, or tax professional, can help your family navigate complex financial and legal decisions after your passing. This ensures your estate is handled according to your wishes and minimizes errors or delays.

Example:
- Work with an estate attorney to oversee the distribution of your assets.
- Hire a financial planner to help your spouse or children invest life insurance benefits wisely.

Benefits:
- Provides expert guidance on tax implications, asset management, and investments.
- Eases the burden on your family by reducing the complexity of managing your estate.

Tip:
Introduce your family to your advisor(s) during your lifetime to establish trust and familiarity.

Chapter 11: Ensuring Financial Wellness for Generations

Building a Legacy with W.E.A.L.T.H.

Creating a lasting legacy isn't just about money—it's about fostering *W.E.A.L.T.H.*: **Wisdom, Education, Assets, Leadership, Trust, and Harmony.** These pillars ensure your family inherits not just resources, but the values and knowledge to sustain and grow them.

Why W.E.A.L.T.H. Matters

Share financial lessons, teach money management, and invest in sustainable assets like property or trusts. Open communication and thoughtful planning foster unity, protecting your family's future while aligning with shared goals.

Legacy in Action

Families like the Carters turned education and leadership into generational success. By sharing knowledge and setting clear plans, they built wealth and strengthened family bonds, leaving a meaningful legacy.

Your Turn

Start small—share wisdom, teach financial literacy, and lead by example. Every step builds a foundation of opportunity and security, ensuring your family thrives for generations to come. *True wealth is the legacy of love and preparedness you leave behind.*

51. Establish Multi-Generational Wealth With Whole Life Insurance: Build Lasting Financial Security

Explanation:
Whole life insurance provides lifelong coverage and builds cash value over time, which can be accessed for various purposes. Using whole life policies strategically can create wealth that passes from one generation to the next, ensuring financial security for your family.

Example:
Purchase a $1 million whole life insurance policy and structure a trust to manage the payout. The trust can invest the proceeds and distribute funds to future generations for education, business ventures, or other needs.

Benefits:
- Guarantees a financial safety net for multiple generations.
- Creates a legacy that aligns with your family's values and goals.

Tip:
Work with a financial planner or estate attorney to design a plan that ensures the wealth is preserved and used responsibly.

52. Gift Annual Premiums for Policies on Your Children: Start Their Coverage Early

Explanation:
Paying the premiums for life insurance policies on your children provides them with long-term financial protection and cash value growth. Starting early ensures lower premiums and builds wealth over time.

Example:
Gift $1,500 annually to pay for a whole life policy on your child, which could grow into a significant asset they can use for emergencies, retirement, or other financial goals.

Benefits:
- Provides your children with financial security throughout their lives.
- Allows them to access cash value as they age for personal or family needs.

Tip:
Set up a policy with flexible payment options to allow your children to take over the premiums when they're financially able.

53. Ensure Retirement Funds for Your Spouse: Supplement Social Security or Pensions

Explanation:
Life insurance proceeds can serve as a safety net for your spouse's retirement, supplementing Social Security benefits, pensions, or personal savings. This ensures they maintain their standard of living.

Example:
Purchase a $500,000 life insurance policy to provide your spouse with additional income during retirement. The funds could be used for living expenses, healthcare, or travel.

Benefits:

- Ensures your spouse doesn't outlive their retirement savings.
- Provides financial stability and peace of mind during their golden years.

Tip:
Consider inflation and rising healthcare costs when calculating the amount needed to support your spouse's retirement.

54. Offer Down-Payment Assistance for Future Homes: Help Family Members Build Stability

Explanation:
Homeownership is a critical step toward financial stability and wealth-building. Allocating part of your life insurance benefits for down-payment assistance helps your family members achieve this milestone.

Example:
Set aside $50,000 from your life insurance policy to assist each child or grandchild with purchasing their first home. Specify the terms for accessing the funds, such as matching contributions or timing.

Benefits:
- Provides a meaningful boost to help family members achieve homeownership.
- Encourages financial responsibility by reducing the need for excessive borrowing.

Tip:
Discuss this plan with your family to ensure they understand the purpose and conditions of the assistance.

55. Provide for Family Travel or Reunions: Ensure Bonds Remain Strong

Explanation:
Setting aside funds for family travel or reunions fosters connection and creates cherished memories. Life insurance benefits or a family fund can cover these expenses, ensuring your family stays united across generations.

Example:
Allocate $20,000 from your policy for an annual family reunion, covering travel, accommodations, and activities. This could include renting a vacation home or funding trips to locations with family significance.

Benefits:
- Strengthens family bonds and traditions.
- Allows loved ones to reconnect and honor your legacy together.

Tip:
Work with family members to plan meaningful events and ensure the funds are used for activities that align with your shared values.

Chapter 12: Reducing the Burden of Final Expenses

Planning Final Expenses: A Lasting Gift of Love

Talking about end-of-life costs may not be easy, but it's one of the most meaningful steps you can take for your loved ones. Funeral costs, medical bills, and legal fees can quickly add up, leaving your family emotionally and financially strained. By planning ahead, you ease that burden, allowing them to focus on cherishing memories instead of worrying about expenses.

Why It Matters

End-of-life planning is an act of love and foresight. Without a plan, final expenses can range from $8,000 to $15,000 or more, catching families off guard during an already difficult time. Taking proactive steps shows care and ensures your family's well-being.

Simple Steps to Ease the Burden

1. **Get Final Expense Insurance:** Affordable policies specifically cover end-of-life costs.
2. **Communicate Your Wishes:** Document your preferences for a funeral, cremation, or memorial to guide your loved ones.

Planning ahead reduces financial stress and provides your family with clarity and peace of mind. It allows them to focus on celebrating your life, not managing unexpected expenses. This simple, thoughtful preparation is a lasting gift, ensuring your legacy is one of love, foresight, and generosity.

56. Specify Headstone and Burial Costs in Your Policy: Eliminate Guesswork

Explanation:
Including headstone and burial costs in your life insurance or final expense policy ensures these details are financially covered. This helps your loved ones avoid guessing about your preferences or worrying about the expense.

Example:
- Allocate $5,000 to $10,000 in your policy for a headstone, burial plot, and installation.
- Provide specific details about the design and inscription to reflect your wishes.

Benefits:
- Removes the emotional and financial burden of making these decisions.
- Ensures your headstone and burial reflect your values and preferences.

Tip:
Document your choices in your funeral plan and share this information with your executor or beneficiary.

57. Cover Memorial Service Expenses: Include Venue, Catering, and Flowers

Explanation:
Memorial services can be costly, including venue rental, catering, flowers, and other arrangements. Setting aside funds ensures your family can hold a meaningful service without financial strain.

Example:
Allocate $10,000 in your policy to cover:

- Venue rental for the service.
- Catering for attendees.
- Floral arrangements and decorations.

Benefits:

- Allows your family to focus on celebrating your life rather than worrying about costs.
- Ensures the service reflects your personality and values.

Tip:
Include specific wishes for your memorial service (e.g., location, music, or theme) in your funeral plan.

58. Set Aside Travel Funds for Attending Family: Make It Easier for Loved Ones to Gather

Explanation:
Travel expenses can prevent some family members from attending your funeral or memorial service. Including travel funds in your plan ensures everyone has the opportunity to say goodbye and support one another.

Example:
- Allocate $5,000-$7,000 to assist family members with airfare, accommodations, or transportation costs.
- Specify a trusted family member to manage the distribution of travel funds.

Benefits:
- Ensures distant relatives can attend and participate in honoring your memory.
- Encourages family connection and support during a difficult time.

Tip:
Inform your executor or beneficiary about your intent to use funds for travel assistance and provide a list of key family members.

59. Plan for Legal Fees Associated With Settling Your Estate: Avoid Surprises

Explanation:
Settling an estate often involves legal fees for probate, executor compensation, and other administrative tasks. Including these costs in your life insurance policy ensures your heirs are not surprised by these expenses.

Example:
- Set aside $10,000-$20,000 to cover attorney fees, court costs, and executor expenses.
- Specify this allocation in your estate plan to clarify its purpose.

Benefits:
- Ensures the estate is settled efficiently and according to your wishes.
- Prevents your heirs from having to cover legal fees out of pocket.

Tip:
Work with an estate attorney to estimate these fees based on the complexity of your estate.

60. Ensure Transportation of Remains If Needed: Include Costs for Relocation

Explanation:
If you pass away far from home or wish to be buried in a specific location, transporting your remains can be expensive. Including these costs in your policy ensures this process is financially covered.

Example:
- Allocate $3,000-$5,000 for the transportation of your remains via air or ground.
- Specify your desired burial location or arrangements for scattering ashes.

Benefits:
- Provides clarity and financial support for your family to fulfill your wishes.
- Eliminates logistical and financial barriers to honoring your preferred final resting place.

Tip:
Discuss your transportation preferences with your family and include details in your funeral plan.

Chapter 13: *Teaching Financial Preparedness*

Teaching financial preparedness isn't just about managing money—it's about creating a foundation of financial security and independence that benefits your loved ones for generations. By equipping them with the skills to earn, save, budget, and invest, you're providing tools that go far beyond dollars and cents. These lessons foster confidence, stability, and resilience, ensuring they are prepared for life's financial challenges. Start with simple, practical steps: involve children in grocery budgeting, guide teenagers in dividing allowances into spending, saving, and giving, or host family discussions about setting and achieving financial goals.

Empowering others with financial knowledge is one of the greatest gifts you can give. Use tools like budgeting apps, investment platforms, and educational resources to make financial literacy accessible and engaging. Show the value of goal-setting and delayed gratification, like saving for a family vacation or building an emergency fund, to teach the power of patience and intentional choices. By normalizing these conversations, you create a culture of transparency and trust, ensuring your financial wisdom becomes a legacy of empowerment, security, and opportunity for generations to come.

61. Teach Your Children About Life Insurance: Help Them Understand Its Value

Explanation:
Life insurance is a critical tool for protecting loved ones and building financial security. Educating your children about its purpose and benefits helps them understand how it can safeguard their families and future.

Example:
- Explain how your life insurance policy ensures your family won't face financial hardship if something happens to you.
- Show them the role life insurance plays in estate planning or funding major expenses like education or homeownership.

Benefits:
- Helps them see life insurance as a practical tool rather than an unnecessary expense.
- Prepares them to make informed decisions about their own policies in adulthood.

Tip:
Encourage them to explore affordable term policies early, especially if they're starting a family or buying a home.

62. Encourage Budgeting and Saving Early: Financial Literacy Is a Gift

Explanation:
Teaching your children how to budget and save equips them with essential skills for financial independence. This foundation helps them manage their finances effectively throughout their lives.

Example:
- Introduce a budgeting app or spreadsheet to track income and expenses.
- Encourage saving a portion of their allowance or first paycheck for short-term and long-term goals.

Benefits:
- Instills habits that reduce debt and increase financial stability.
- Helps them prioritize needs over wants and prepare for future goals.

Tip:
Lead by example by sharing how you budget for household expenses and save for emergencies or retirement.

63. Show Them How to Invest Wisely: Set the Example With Your Policies

Explanation:
Teaching your children about investing helps them grow their wealth and achieve financial goals. Use your own life insurance policies, retirement accounts, or investments as teaching tools to demonstrate the power of compounding and diversification.

Example:
- Show them how your permanent life insurance policy's cash value grows over time.
- Discuss the importance of diversifying investments to balance risk and reward.

Benefits:
- Prepares them to make confident, informed investment decisions.
- Encourages long-term thinking and planning for financial security.

Tip:
Encourage them to start with low-cost index funds or employer-sponsored retirement accounts to build a strong foundation.

64. Discuss Emergency Planning Openly: Normalize Preparation

Explanation:
Emergencies are inevitable, but planning for them reduces stress and financial impact. Teaching your children about emergency funds and contingency plans normalizes preparation as a responsible habit.

Example:
- Share how you've set up an emergency fund covering 3-6 months of living expenses.
- Discuss how life insurance provides financial support in unforeseen situations, such as accidents or illness.

Benefits:
- Encourages proactive financial planning.
- Reduces anxiety about potential emergencies by showing they can be managed effectively.

Tip:
Help them start their own emergency fund by setting a savings goal and contributing small, consistent amounts.

65. Pass Down a Philosophy of Financial Responsibility: Lead by Example

Explanation:
Your actions speak louder than words. By demonstrating financial responsibility in your own life, you inspire your children to adopt similar habits and values.

Example:
- Show how you prioritize saving for retirement, paying off debt, and investing in your family's future.
- Share stories about financial mistakes you've learned from to provide relatable lessons.

Benefits:
- Instills a mindset of accountability and thoughtful decision-making.
- Helps them see financial responsibility as a path to freedom and stability.

Tip:
Use family meetings or casual conversations to share your financial philosophy and encourage open discussions about money.

Chapter 14: *Preserving Your Memory*

Imagine your loved ones reflecting on your life with admiration and gratitude, feeling deeply connected to your values and the impact you had on them. Preserving your memory goes beyond material assets; it's about leaving an enduring legacy of your stories, wisdom, and traditions.

Handwritten letters, photo albums, or cherished mementos carry immense sentimental value. Picture a grandchild discovering a letter filled with your wisdom and encouragement, feeling your presence even in your absence. Additionally, pass down family traditions, recipes, or rituals that infuse everyday moments with your spirit, keeping your memory alive in the rhythms of their lives.

Whether it's funding a scholarship, planting a commemorative garden, or supporting a cause close to your heart, these actions allow your values to live on. Combine this with modern tools like digital archives or family history platforms to share your photos, writings, and stories across generations.

66. Create a Family Video Library: Share Stories, Wisdom, and Laughter

Explanation:
A family video library preserves your stories, memories, and personality for future generations. Videos allow your loved ones to see and hear you, adding a personal and emotional connection to your legacy.

Example:
- Record videos of yourself sharing family history, life lessons, and personal values.
- Include footage of everyday moments, special occasions, or messages for future milestones like weddings or graduations.

Benefits:
- Offers a visual and emotional connection for future generations.
- Captures your voice, expressions, and wisdom in a lasting format.

Tip:
Organize the videos into themes (e.g., "Life Lessons," "Family Stories") and store them digitally on a secure platform that family members can access.

67. Host a Living Celebration: Share Love and Gratitude While Alive

Explanation:
A living celebration is a joyful gathering that allows you to express gratitude and appreciation for your loved ones while you're alive. It's an opportunity to create lasting memories in a positive and uplifting environment.

Example:
- Host a dinner, picnic, or party where you share heartfelt messages of appreciation with your family and friends.
- Include meaningful activities, such as storytelling, photo slideshows, or a "memory jar" where guests write down their favorite moments with you.

Benefits:
- Strengthens relationships and brings closure to unspoken sentiments.
- Allows you to celebrate your life and the people who matter most to you.

Tip:
Make the event as formal or casual as you'd like, and consider involving family members in planning to make it special.

68. Plant a Tree in Your Honor: A Living Symbol of Your Legacy

Explanation:
Planting a tree in your honor creates a lasting, living tribute that represents growth, resilience, and the impact you've had on your family and the world.

Example:
- Plant a tree in your backyard or at a meaningful location like a family property or community park.
- Choose a species with symbolic meaning, such as an oak for strength or a flowering cherry for beauty and renewal.

Benefits:
- Provides a tangible, enduring symbol of your legacy.
- Acts as a gathering place for family members to reflect and reconnect.

Tip:
Include a plaque or marker with your name and a meaningful quote to personalize the tribute.

69. Write a Book or Memoir: Document Your Life Lessons

Explanation:
A memoir allows you to share your life story, experiences, and lessons in your own words. It's a timeless way to preserve your legacy and provide guidance for your descendants.

Example:
- Write about key moments in your life, such as overcoming challenges, finding love, or pursuing your passions.
- Share practical wisdom, like financial lessons, relationship advice, or career insights.

Benefits:
- Provides future generations with a personal and inspiring connection to your life.
- Creates a permanent record of your journey and values.

Tip:
If writing feels daunting, consider working with a ghostwriter or using memoir-writing prompts to structure your story.

70. Dedicate a Family Tradition in Your Name: Keep Your Memory Alive Through Shared Experiences

Explanation:
Creating a family tradition ensures your legacy is celebrated regularly. It brings loved ones together and keeps your memory alive in a positive, meaningful way.

Example:
- Dedicate an annual family reunion or holiday celebration to your honor.
- Start a unique tradition, like a "Family Gratitude Day," where everyone shares what they're thankful for.

Benefits:
- Strengthens family bonds through shared activities.
- Provides a consistent way to honor your life and values.

Tip:
Choose a tradition that aligns with your personality or passions, making it easier for your family to carry it forward.

Chapter 15: *Passing on Values Alongside Wealth*

When leaving a legacy, wealth without wisdom can be fleeting. The greatest inheritance is a foundation of shared values that amplify and sustain the material wealth you pass down. Start by defining your core values—like generosity, resilience, or hard work—and weave them into your family's story. Teach by example, sharing stories of challenges and triumphs to illustrate the principles that guided your life.

Use wealth as a tool to reinforce values. Establish scholarships, fund family ventures, or support charitable causes tied to your priorities. Open communication is key—share your financial plans and the "why" behind them, helping loved ones understand their role as stewards of both resources and principles.

Celebrate shared traditions and encourage financial literacy to ensure future generations carry your legacy with confidence and purpose. A personal letter with your estate plans can express your hopes, lessons, and dreams, creating a guiding light for your family.

71. Tie Insurance Benefits to Meaningful Goals: Encourage Recipients to Use Funds for Education, Homeownership, or Investments

Explanation:
Life insurance benefits can be a powerful tool for improving your family's future. By attaching specific goals to the funds, you help your beneficiaries use them purposefully and wisely.

Example:
- Encourage your children to use a portion of the payout for higher education or professional certifications.
- Specify that part of the funds should go toward a first-time homebuyer down payment or starting a business.
- Suggest investing the money to build long-term financial security.

Benefits:
- Provides clear direction for using the funds in a way that aligns with your values.
- Reduces the likelihood of misuse or squandering the inheritance.

Tip:
Communicate your goals with your beneficiaries and include a written note explaining your intentions.

72. Include a Letter of Intent With Your Insurance Policy: Explain Your Hopes for How the Money Will Be Used

Explanation:
A letter of intent is a personal message that accompanies your life insurance policy. It provides context for your decisions and expresses your hopes for how the benefits will be used.

Example:
"Dear Family,
This policy is my gift to you, meant to provide stability and opportunity. I hope it will help with college tuition, homeownership, or investments to secure your future. Remember, this is not just money but a representation of my love and belief in your potential."

Benefits:
- Adds a personal touch to your financial legacy.
- Encourages beneficiaries to use the funds responsibly and thoughtfully.

Tip:
Store the letter with your policy documents and share its location with your executor or trusted family member.

73. Establish a Family Mission Statement: Use Your Legacy to Reflect Shared Values

Explanation:
A family mission statement defines your collective values and goals, creating a unified vision for how your legacy will be carried forward. It serves as a guide for decision-making and actions.

Example:
"Our family mission is to prioritize education, support each other through challenges, and contribute to our community by giving back. We will use the resources left to us to continue building a legacy of love, responsibility, and growth."

Benefits:
- Strengthens family identity and purpose.
- Ensures your legacy reflects shared values across generations.

Tip:
Involve family members in drafting the mission statement to encourage buy-in and commitment.

74. Encourage Philanthropy With a Portion of the Benefits: Teach the Importance of Giving Back

Explanation:
Setting aside a portion of your insurance benefits for charitable giving reinforces the value of generosity and community impact. This can be done individually by beneficiaries or through a family foundation.

Example:
- Allocate 10% of the insurance payout to a cause you're passionate about, such as education, healthcare, or environmental conservation.
- Encourage family members to decide collectively which charities to support annually.

Benefits:
- Inspires a legacy of philanthropy and compassion.
- Strengthens family bonds through shared acts of giving.

Tip:
Discuss the importance of giving back with your family and include suggestions for potential causes or organizations in your estate plan.

75. Create a Family Trust Fund With Guidelines for Use: Ensure Your Wealth Supports Future Generations Responsibly

Explanation:
A family trust fund is a structured way to manage and distribute your wealth over time. By setting clear guidelines, you can ensure the funds are used to support meaningful goals and prevent misuse.

Example:
- Establish a trust fund with rules such as:
    - Funds can only be used for education, first homes, or starting a business.
    - Distributions are contingent on reaching milestones, such as graduating college or maintaining employment.

Benefits:
- Protects your wealth from being squandered or mismanaged.
- Provides long-term support for multiple generations.

Tip:
Work with an estate attorney to set up the trust and ensure the guidelines align with your values and goals.

Chapter 16: *Empowering Your Beneficiaries*

Passing on wealth is an act of love and trust, but true empowerment means equipping beneficiaries with the knowledge and tools to manage their inheritance wisely. Start with financial education—teach budgeting, investing, and long-term planning, and connect them with resources like books or advisors to guide informed decisions.

Transparency *is key. Share your estate plans and the values behind your decisions to foster trust and clarity. Structured plans, like trusts with milestone-based disbursements, promote responsible financial behavior and encourage long-term growth.*

*Finally, pair resources with **values**. Inspire responsibility, philanthropy, and unity by sharing your principles and leading by example. Encourage gratitude and stewardship, helping beneficiaries see their inheritance as a tool for growth, purpose, and positive impact. By doing so, your legacy becomes a springboard for their dreams and a reflection of your enduring love.*

76. Prepare Your Family to Handle Life Insurance Claims: Provide Step-by-Step Instructions

Explanation:
Filing a life insurance claim can be an unfamiliar and overwhelming process during a difficult time. By providing clear, written instructions, you simplify the process for your beneficiaries, ensuring they can access the funds without delays.

Example Instructions:
1. Locate the policy document and contact the insurance company.
2. Provide the policy number and details about the insured (e.g., date of birth and death).
3. Submit required documents, including a certified death certificate.
4. Choose a payment option (lump sum or installments).

Benefits:
- Prevents delays or errors during the claims process.
- Gives your family peace of mind during an emotional time.

Tip:
Store these instructions with your policy and ensure a trusted family member knows where to find them.

77. Teach Them About Tax Implications of Receiving Benefits: Help Them Plan Wisely

Explanation:
While life insurance payouts are generally tax-free, certain scenarios—like interest payments or large estates—can create tax implications. Educating your family helps them prepare for any potential liabilities.

Example:
- Explain that the death benefit is usually tax-free but interest earned on delayed payouts might be taxable.
- Discuss estate tax thresholds if your total estate value exceeds federal or state limits.

Benefits:
- Helps your beneficiaries make informed financial decisions.
- Prevents unexpected tax burdens that could reduce the payout.

Tip:
Include a consultation with a tax professional as part of your legacy planning to clarify tax scenarios for your heirs.

78. Appoint a Financial Advisor to Guide Them: Ensure They Have Support for Smart Decisions

Explanation:
A financial advisor can help your family manage life insurance proceeds effectively. This includes budgeting, investing, and planning for long-term goals.

Example:
- Appoint a financial advisor to assist your spouse or children with managing large payouts.
- The advisor can create a plan for investing the money, covering debts, or funding education.

Benefits:
- Provides expert guidance, reducing the risk of poor financial decisions.
- Helps your family make the most of the funds while aligning with their financial goals.

Tip:
Introduce your family to the advisor during your lifetime to build trust and familiarity.

79. Include Beneficiaries in Legacy Planning Discussions: Foster Transparency and Trust

Explanation:
Involving your beneficiaries in legacy planning discussions ensures they understand your intentions and how they fit into the overall plan. This transparency reduces misunderstandings and fosters trust among family members.

Example:
- Discuss how you'd like the life insurance benefits to be used, such as paying off debts, funding education, or starting a business.
- Share your reasons for distributing assets as outlined in your will or trust.

Benefits:
- Encourages open communication and reduces potential disputes.
- Ensures your beneficiaries are aligned with your vision for your legacy.

Tip:
Hold family meetings to discuss your plans, allowing beneficiaries to ask questions and express concerns.

80. Ensure They Understand Your Life Insurance Policy Details: Avoid Confusion or Missed Opportunities

Explanation:
Life insurance policies can be complex, with varying terms, riders, and conditions. Ensuring your beneficiaries understand the details helps them maximize the benefits and avoid mistakes.

Example:
- Explain the type of policy you have (e.g., term or whole life) and its payout structure.
- Highlight any additional riders, such as critical illness or accidental death benefits, that they should be aware of.

Benefits:
- Prevents beneficiaries from overlooking benefits or misunderstanding coverage.
- Reduces confusion during the claims process.

Tip:
Create a summary of your policy's key details and review it with your beneficiaries to clarify any questions.

Chapter 17: *Long-Term Impact Through Life Insurance*

Life insurance isn't just about financial security—it's about creating a lasting legacy. By aligning your policy with your priorities, you can leave a meaningful imprint on the lives of those you love. Let's explore the acronym *IMPACT* to see how life insurance helps build a legacy of lasting significance.

I – Income Replacement
Life insurance ensures your family's financial stability by replacing lost income.

M – Memorializing Your Legacy
Use life insurance to fund projects that reflect your passions, like scholarships or charitable initiatives.

P – Planning for Generational Wealth
The death benefit creates opportunities for long-term prosperity.

A – Addressing Debt and Final Expenses
Life insurance relieves your family of debts, mortgages, and final expenses like funeral costs, allowing them to focus on healing rather than financial logistics.

C – Covering Educational Needs
Education transforms lives. Your policy can fund tuition or training, empowering your loved ones to pursue their dreams without financial strain.

T – Tax Advantages
Life insurance benefits are typically tax-free, maximizing the value passed to your heirs and enhancing your estate planning strategy.

81. Set Up Policies for Younger Family Members: Protect Them While Building Cash Value

Explanation:
Purchasing life insurance for younger family members, such as children or grandchildren, provides them with lifelong coverage and builds cash value that can be accessed in the future.

Example:

- Purchase a whole life policy for your grandchild with a $50,000 death benefit. The cash value can grow over time, and the policyholder can access it for college tuition, a wedding, or starting a business.

Benefits:

- Locks in lower premiums due to their young age and good health.
- Creates a financial safety net for their future.

Tip:
Transfer ownership of the policy to them when they reach adulthood, ensuring they continue to benefit from it.

82. Use Life Insurance as a Retirement Tool: Policies With Living Benefits Can Supplement Income

Explanation:
Some permanent life insurance policies offer living benefits, allowing you to access the cash value or death benefit while still alive. This can provide supplemental income during retirement.

Example:
- Use the cash value of a whole life policy to cover unexpected medical expenses or to supplement your Social Security income.
- Access a portion of the death benefit early via a rider if you face a chronic illness.

Benefits:
- Provides financial flexibility during retirement.
- Helps cover expenses without depleting other savings or investments.

Tip:
Work with a financial advisor to understand the tax implications and ensure withdrawals align with your retirement plan.

83. Create a Lasting Charitable Endowment: Use Your Policy to Fund Causes You Care About

Explanation:
Designating a portion of your life insurance benefits to create a charitable endowment ensures your values and philanthropic goals live on. This approach supports causes you care about for years to come.

Example:

- Name a nonprofit organization as the beneficiary of a $100,000 life insurance policy. The endowment can generate annual income to fund scholarships or community programs.
- Alternatively, allocate a percentage of your benefits to establish a family foundation that oversees charitable contributions.

Benefits:

- Creates a meaningful, long-term impact on your community or chosen cause.
- Inspires future generations to continue your philanthropic legacy.

Tip:
Consult with the organization to ensure your gift aligns with their mission and operational structure.

84. Provide for Unexpected Expenses for Generations to Come: Build a Financial Cushion

Explanation:
Life insurance benefits can serve as a financial cushion for your family, helping them navigate unexpected challenges such as medical emergencies, natural disasters, or economic downturns.

Example:
- Allocate a portion of the benefits to a family trust fund specifically earmarked for emergencies. This ensures that funds are available for unforeseen circumstances without disrupting other financial goals.

Benefits:
- Provides peace of mind for your loved ones.
- Helps maintain family stability during difficult times.

Tip:
Set clear guidelines for when and how funds can be accessed to ensure they're used appropriately.

85. Turn Insurance Benefits Into Investment Opportunities: Encourage Heirs to Grow the Wealth You Leave Behind

Explanation:
Using life insurance benefits as seed money for investments can help your heirs build and grow their wealth over time. This approach turns your legacy into a foundation for future financial success.

Example:
- Encourage your beneficiaries to invest part of their inheritance in diversified portfolios, real estate, or starting a business.
- Provide guidance through a letter of intent or family mission statement to ensure the funds are used thoughtfully.

Benefits:
- Promotes financial literacy and independence.
- Multiplies the impact of your legacy by creating additional opportunities for growth.

Tip:
Consider partnering with a financial advisor to help beneficiaries develop an investment strategy aligned with their goals.

Chapter 18: *The Role of Communication in Legacy Planning*

Legacy planning isn't just about assets—it's about creating clarity and unity. Without open communication, even well-designed plans can lead to confusion or conflict. By sharing your intentions and values, you transform your legacy into an act of love, providing peace of mind for your family.

Starting the Conversation
Approach the topic with honesty and kindness, saying, *"I want to ensure our family understands my wishes."* Discuss your values, asset distribution, roles, and final wishes in a calm, open setting. Encourage questions to foster understanding and trust.

Building a Legacy of Love
Clear communication eliminates uncertainty, strengthens bonds, and ensures your family focuses on honoring your life—not unraveling your plans. Whether through a family meeting, a heartfelt letter, or a video message, your openness helps preserve unity and clarity.

By taking the time to talk about your plans, you leave more than instructions—you leave a legacy of connection, compassion, and understanding that will resonate through generations.

86. Discuss Your Plans Openly With Loved Ones: Eliminate Uncertainty and Misunderstanding

Explanation:
Openly discussing your plans helps your family understand your intentions and ensures there are no surprises. Clear communication reduces the risk of conflict and ensures your wishes are honored.

Example:
- Share your estate planning decisions, such as how assets will be divided or the purpose of specific allocations (e.g., for education or charitable giving).
- Explain the reasoning behind your choices, such as naming certain beneficiaries or setting up a trust.

Benefits:
- Builds trust and clarity among family members.
- Helps manage expectations and reduces potential disputes.

Tip:
Choose a calm, private setting for these conversations and allow time for questions.

87. Host a Family Legacy Meeting: Share Your Intentions and Invite Questions

Explanation:
A family legacy meeting is a formal gathering where you discuss your plans, share your vision for the future, and address any questions or concerns. This ensures everyone is informed and aligned with your goals.

Example:
- Present an overview of your estate plan, including major assets, life insurance benefits, and any trusts or endowments.
- Share your family mission statement and discuss how the funds or resources should support your shared values.

Benefits:
- Provides a platform for open dialogue and transparency.
- Strengthens family bonds and creates a sense of shared purpose.

Tip:
Include your financial advisor or attorney in the meeting to provide professional clarity and answer technical questions.

88. Write a "Legacy Letter" for Family Members: Personalize Your Messages to Each Recipient

Explanation:
A legacy letter is a heartfelt message that conveys your love, wisdom, and hopes for each family member. These letters provide a personal connection that lasts beyond your lifetime.

Example:

- For a child: *"I'm so proud of the person you've become. Always remember to follow your dreams and trust in your abilities. I hope this gift supports you in creating a life filled with joy and purpose."*
- For a grandchild: *"Use these funds to invest in your education or pursue your passions. You have so much potential, and I believe in you completely."*

Benefits:

- Offers emotional support and encouragement.
- Makes your legacy feel personal and meaningful.

Tip:
Store your letters with your estate documents or deliver them during a living celebration.

89. Encourage Feedback During Planning: Let Family Members Feel Involved in the Process

Explanation:
Inviting feedback from your family ensures your plans align with their needs and perspectives. It also fosters a sense of inclusion and collaboration, strengthening their connection to your legacy.

Example:

- Ask for input on how to allocate family trust funds (e.g., for education, business ventures, or emergency use).
- Discuss preferences for family traditions or philanthropic goals tied to your estate.

Benefits:

- Encourages family members to take ownership of their roles in your legacy.
- Builds understanding and consensus, reducing the likelihood of future disagreements.

Tip:
Host follow-up meetings to address new concerns or adapt plans as circumstances change.

90. Create a Digital Legacy Plan: Share Access to Important Online Accounts and Documents

Explanation:
A digital legacy plan ensures your family can access your online accounts, including financial platforms, email, social media, and cloud storage. This prevents accounts from being lost or inaccessible after your passing.

Example:
- Use a password manager to securely store login credentials for all your accounts.
- Create a digital document listing key accounts, their purpose, and instructions for managing or closing them.

Benefits:
- Simplifies account management for your family or executor.
- Prevents loss of valuable digital assets, such as photos, documents, or cryptocurrency.

Tip:
Designate a trusted family member or executor to manage your digital assets, and ensure they understand their responsibilities.

Chapter 19: *Leaving a Lasting Emotional Impact*

Leaving a Lasting Emotional Legacy

A true legacy isn't just about wealth—it's about the love, values, and connections you leave behind. Your presence continues through the stories shared, the traditions upheld, and the lessons passed down.

Why Emotional Impact Matters

Emotional legacies provide comfort and inspiration. A kind word, shared memory, or guiding value can uplift loved ones far beyond material gifts. It's how you make them feel that truly lasts.

Creating an Emotional Legacy

- *Share your stories:* Capture life lessons in letters or videos.
- *Express love and gratitude:* Affirm your care through heartfelt words.
- *Pass down traditions:* Teach family recipes or create meaningful rituals.
- *Instill values:* Inspire future generations with your principles.

Your emotional legacy is the love and wisdom you leave *within* your family—a gift that endures forever.

91. Write Goodbye Letters for Significant Life Milestones: Birthdays, Weddings, or Other Key Moments

Explanation:
Goodbye letters for major milestones provide heartfelt guidance and encouragement for your loved ones during important moments in their lives. These letters are a way to remain present in their journeys, even if you're no longer physically there.

Example:

- **For a wedding:** *"Today is one of the most joyful days of your life, and though I can't be there in person, know that I am with you in spirit. Marriage is a partnership built on love, trust, and laughter. Cherish each other."*
- **For a birthday:** *"Happy 18th birthday! This is the start of an incredible journey. Follow your dreams boldly and always believe in yourself. I'm so proud of you."*

Benefits:

- Provides emotional support and wisdom tailored to each milestone.
- Creates a sense of connection and presence during life's big events.

Tip:
Store these letters with your will or in a legacy binder and ensure your family knows when to deliver them.

92. Create a Time Capsule With Personal Mementos: Include Photos, Letters, and Cherished Items

Explanation:
A time capsule preserves your memories, stories, and treasures for future generations to discover. It's a fun and meaningful way to share your life's journey and values.

Example:
- Include personal letters, family photos, and mementos like a favorite book, recipe, or small trinkets.
- Add a handwritten note explaining the significance of each item and your hopes for the family's future.

Benefits:
- Provides a tangible connection to your life and legacy.
- Inspires curiosity and appreciation for family history.

Tip:
Bury or store the time capsule in a safe, memorable location and provide instructions for when it should be opened (e.g., a specific anniversary or milestone).

93. Start a Family Tradition in Your Honor: Let Your Memory Live On in Shared Rituals

Explanation:
A family tradition is a recurring activity or event that strengthens bonds and keeps your memory alive. By dedicating a tradition in your honor, you ensure your values and presence remain a part of your family's life.

Example:
- Start a yearly family camping trip, Sunday dinner, or game night in your name.
- Dedicate a "Day of Service" where family members volunteer in your honor.

Benefits:
- Strengthens family connections through shared experiences.
- Keeps your memory alive in a joyful, meaningful way.

Tip:
Choose a tradition that reflects your passions or personality, making it easy and enjoyable for your family to continue.

94. Record Your Voice or Create Videos: Hearing and Seeing You Will Bring Comfort to Your Loved Ones

Explanation:
Hearing your voice and seeing your expressions in videos provides comfort and emotional connection for your loved ones. These recordings preserve your personality, humor, and wisdom.

Example:
- Record personal messages for family members or advice for life's challenges.
- Share your favorite jokes, songs, or stories from your life.

Benefits:
- Creates a vivid, lasting reminder of your presence.
- Offers emotional reassurance during difficult moments.

Tip:
Store these recordings digitally for easy access and share them during family gatherings or milestones.

95. Celebrate Life's Milestones Together While You Can: Leave No Regrets in the Hearts of Those You Love

Explanation:
Celebrating milestones with your loved ones while you're alive ensures that you're part of their joyful moments and memories. It also strengthens relationships and reduces future regrets.

Example:
- Attend graduations, weddings, and other special events.
- Plan family vacations or dinners to celebrate achievements together.

Benefits:
- Fosters deeper connections and joyful memories.
- Ensures your presence in significant family moments.

Tip:
Prioritize quality time and actively participate in celebrations, big or small.

Chapter 20: Planning Beyond Your Lifetime

Planning beyond your lifetime is an act of love and vision. It's about ensuring your values, resources, and priorities continue to positively shape the lives of your loved ones and the causes you care about. Thoughtful planning creates clarity, avoids confusion, and provides stability for future generations.

Start with a comprehensive estate plan that includes a will, trusts, and healthcare directives. Consider using life insurance or charitable funds to support legacy projects like scholarships or community programs. Beyond financial assets, leave a lasting emotional impact by documenting your life's lessons, values, and hopes for your family.

Communicating your plans is just as important as creating them. Share your wishes openly with loved ones to ensure they understand your intentions and feel connected to your legacy. Organize essential documents in a secure, accessible location for a seamless transition when the time comes.

By planning today, you're leaving more than an inheritance—you're creating a legacy of love, purpose, and inspiration that will guide and uplift generations to come.

96. Update Your Policies After Major Life Changes: Marriage, Divorce, Births, or Deaths

Explanation:
Major life events can significantly affect your estate and insurance plans. Regularly updating your policies ensures they reflect your current relationships and intentions.

Example:
- Add a new spouse or child as a beneficiary after marriage or birth.
- Remove an ex-spouse after divorce.
- Adjust coverage amounts to account for new financial responsibilities, such as supporting a growing family.

Benefits:
- Ensures your plans remain relevant and aligned with your wishes.
- Prevents legal disputes or unintended distributions.

Tip:
Review your policies annually or after any significant life event to ensure accuracy.

97. Designate Contingent Beneficiaries: Ensure Funds Are Distributed Even If Primary Beneficiaries Are Unavailable

Explanation:
A contingent beneficiary is a backup who receives benefits if the primary beneficiary is unable to do so. This step ensures your assets are distributed as intended, even in unforeseen circumstances.

Example:
- Name your spouse as the primary beneficiary and your child as the contingent.
- If your primary beneficiary predeceases you or cannot claim the funds, the contingent beneficiary will inherit instead.

Benefits:
- Provides a safety net for your plans.
- Reduces the risk of delays or legal complications in distributing benefits.

Tip:
Regularly review both primary and contingent beneficiaries to ensure they remain accurate.

98. Choose a Trusted Executor for Your Will and Policies: Avoid Family Conflict by Selecting Someone Impartial and Capable

Explanation:
The executor is responsible for carrying out your will and managing your estate. Selecting a trustworthy and capable person ensures your wishes are respected and disputes are minimized.

Example:
- Choose a neutral party, such as a lawyer or financial professional, if you anticipate family conflicts.
- Provide them with a detailed list of your assets, policies, and instructions.

Benefits:
- Reduces the potential for mismanagement or disputes among heirs.
- Ensures your estate is settled efficiently and according to your wishes.

Tip:
Discuss the role with your chosen executor beforehand to confirm their willingness and understanding.

99. Consider Legacy Planning With a Professional: Work With an Estate Planner or Financial Advisor to Maximize Your Impact

Explanation:
A professional estate planner or financial advisor can help optimize your legacy, ensuring your assets are distributed efficiently and with minimal tax impact. They can also help structure trusts, endowments, or other long-term financial tools.

Example:
- Work with an estate planner to create a trust that funds scholarships or charitable causes.
- Collaborate with a financial advisor to balance tax efficiency and wealth preservation.

Benefits:
- Ensures your plans are comprehensive and legally sound.
- Maximizes the financial impact of your legacy while reducing potential costs.

Tip:
Choose a professional experienced in estate and legacy planning, and involve your family in the process when appropriate.

100. Leave Clear, Accessible Instructions for Your Plans: Make It Easy for Your Family to Carry Out Your Wishes

Explanation:
Providing clear and accessible instructions ensures your family can quickly and efficiently manage your estate and carry out your plans. This minimizes stress and confusion during an emotional time.

Example:
- Create a legacy binder containing your will, life insurance policies, financial accounts, and funeral preferences.
- Include a step-by-step guide for accessing benefits and managing responsibilities.

Benefits:
- Simplifies the process for your family and executor.
- Reduces the likelihood of missed or mismanaged assets.

Tip:
Keep the binder in a secure, known location, such as a fireproof safe, and inform your executor or family members of its whereabouts.

101. Trust in the Legacy You've Built: Know That Your Careful Planning Will Provide Love, Security, and Peace of Mind for Generations to Come

Explanation:
Once you've created and documented your plans, trust that your thoughtful preparation will support and inspire your loved ones. Your legacy is more than financial—it's the love, values, and guidance you've shared.

Example:
- Reflect on how your efforts will help your family achieve goals like education, homeownership, and philanthropy.
- Take pride in the traditions, letters, and plans you've put in place to keep your memory alive.

Benefits:
- Brings you peace of mind knowing your family is cared for.
- Allows your loved ones to feel supported and connected to your values.

Tip:
Celebrate the legacy you've built by sharing your plans with your family, emphasizing the love and care that inspired your actions.

Conclusion: A Legacy Built on Love and Planning

Your legacy is more than money, assets, or documents—it's the story you leave behind, woven with love, intention, and thoughtfulness. Throughout this journey, we've explored the many facets of legacy-building: from offering emotional gifts that provide comfort and wisdom, to using life insurance and estate planning as tools for financial security and generational impact. Each chapter has underscored the power of combining heartfelt connections with practical preparation.

By prioritizing **emotional impact**, you gift your family the memories, values, and love that will guide them through life's challenges. Through **life insurance and financial planning**, you ensure that their future is free from unnecessary burdens, granting them the stability to thrive. With tools like **estate planning and communication**, you pave the way for clarity and unity, reducing confusion and potential conflict during difficult times.

This legacy of love and planning will resonate far beyond your years, creating ripples of security, guidance, and inspiration for generations to come. It is a reflection of your care, your vision, and your desire to leave the world—and your family—better than you found it.

As you continue this meaningful journey, may you find joy in knowing that every effort you make today is a gift of love that will endure forever.

www.ingramcontent.com/pod-product-compliance
Lightning Source LLC
Chambersburg PA
CBHW071551220526
45469CB00003B/984